AMERICA

America Decides *2024*

Trump vs. Harris - A Defining Choice for the Nation's Future

Lindsey T. Gordon

*AMERICA DECIDES *2024**

COPYRIGHT

All rights reserved. No part of this publication may be reproduced, distributed, or transmitted in any form or by any means, including photocopying, recording, or other electronic or mechanical methods, without the prior written permission of the publisher, except in the case of brief quotations embodied in critical reviews and certain other noncommercial uses permitted by copyright law.

Copyright © Lindsey T. Gordon, 2024.

AMERICA DECIDES *2024*

TABLE OF CONTENTS

INTRODUCTION..............................7
Overview of the 2024 Presidential Election.................................... 7
   The Stakes: What's at Risk for America?...10
   Analyzing the Contenders: Donald Trump and Kamala Harris................ 13

CHAPTER ONE..............................**19**
The Historical Landscape of U.S. Presidential Elections........................... 19
   Key Elections That Defined America's Path................................. 23
   A Review of Election Narratives: Myths and Realities.......................... 29

CHAPTER TWO.............................**34**
The Candidates - Backgrounds, Visions, and Leadership Styles..............34
   Contrasting Leadership Philosophies and Styles................... 42
   Policy Priorities and Vision for America... 46

CHAPTER THREE............................50

The Economy - Competing Plans for
Prosperity... 50

    Economic Theories and Realities: Who
    Has the Stronger Plan?......................60

    Evaluating the Realities and
    Potential Outcomes........................... 64

CHAPTER FOUR............................ 68

Healthcare in America - Access,
Affordability, and Policy Proposals.......68

    Trump's Approach to Healthcare
    and Reform..72

    Harris' Plans for Expanding and
    Reinventing Healthcare.................... 77

CHAPTER FIVE...............................86

Immigration and Border Policies -
Balancing Security and Humanity........ 86

    Harris' Approach to Immigration
    Reform... 92

    The Humanitarian and Economic
    Implications of Border Policies........ 97

CHAPTER SIX............................. 109

National Security and Foreign
Policy - America's Role on the
Global Stage... 109

Harris' Diplomatic Vision: Collaboration and Multilateralism.............................. 113
Key Global Issues: Trade, Climate, and Alliances..................... 117

CHAPTER SEVEN........................ 125
Social Justice and Civil Rights - Defining American Values.................. 125
Harris' History and Policy Goals for Social Equity............................. 129
The Future of Race Relations, Policing, and Equality..................... 133

CHAPTER EIGHT..........................137
The Environment and Climate Change - Competing Visions for Sustainability......................................137
Harris' Commitment to Climate Change Action.................................141
Environmental Policy in an Era of Climate Crisis............................ 146

CHAPTER NINE........................... 151
Education and Workforce Development - Preparing America for Tomorrow.......................................151

Harris' Agenda for Public Education and Workforce Innovation........................ 155
The Role of Federal vs. State Control in Education....................... 159

CHAPTER TEN............................. 165

The Influence of Media, Social Media, and Election Integrity.............. 165
Harris' Media Strategy and Public Engagement.................................... 168
Safeguarding Democracy: Election Security and Misinformation.............................. 171

CONCLUSION...............................176

The Election's Implications for America's Identity and Future............. 176
Where We Stand as a Nation at This Pivotal Moment....................... 178
Looking Beyond 2024: The Long-Term Effects on America's Path.. 180

AMERICA DECIDES *2024*

INTRODUCTION

Overview of the 2024 Presidential Election

The 2024 U.S. presidential election is shaping up to be one of the most consequential in recent history. In an era marked by polarized politics, unprecedented challenges, and rapidly evolving societal dynamics, the upcoming election has captured both national and international attention.

The political landscape in 2024 is defined by a divided country, with tensions surrounding economic inequality, healthcare, climate change, and social justice at an all-time high. The candidates, former President Donald Trump and current Vice President Kamala Harris, represent not just differing policies but starkly contrasting visions for America's future.

Donald Trump's return to the political arena comes with both a controversial legacy and a loyal base that sees him as a champion against the so-called "establishment." His platform often focuses on issues like border security, economic nationalism, and deregulation, appealing to those who feel left behind by globalization and the progressive agenda.

Meanwhile, Kamala Harris, the first female, Black, and South Asian vice president, represents a coalition that envisions a more inclusive, forward-thinking America. Her campaign is built on the principles of social justice, expanding healthcare, and climate action, aimed at addressing systemic inequalities and reasserting America's role as a global leader on issues like climate change and human rights.

The dynamics of this election are further complicated by the post-pandemic economic recovery, cultural debates over the direction of American society, and ongoing concerns over election security and the influence of social media. Voter turnout is expected to be record-breaking, and early polls reveal a deeply divided electorate, where each vote represents not just a preference for policy but a vision for the country's soul. Against this backdrop, the question facing America is more than just who will lead; it's about what kind of nation the United States aspires to be.

The Stakes: What's at Risk for America?

The stakes in the 2024 election extend far beyond the typical political cycle. For many Americans, the choice between Trump and Harris represents a decision about the nation's core values, its standing on the global stage, and the future direction of American democracy. At stake are foundational questions: Will America lean into a future that embraces diversity, collaboration, and global responsibility, or will it pursue a more isolationist, economically protectionist, and traditionalist path?

Economically, this election will define policies on job creation, technological innovation, and trade. Harris' policies lean towards investing in green technology, enhancing worker protections, and expanding access to higher education and job training programs.

Trump's economic vision, by contrast, advocates for energy independence (often via fossil fuels), deregulation to spur business growth, and a nationalist approach to trade. The winner's policies will influence everything from the price of consumer goods to the state of the environment, affecting generations to come.

Socially, this election has profound implications for issues of justice, equity, and human rights. Harris' platform calls for progressive reforms in policing, criminal justice, and racial equity, aiming to create a more just society for historically marginalized communities. Trump's approach prioritizes law and order, traditional values, and a more restrained approach to federal oversight in social matters. These contrasting views encapsulate the cultural divide in America and touch on how Americans see their communities, their freedoms, and the role of government.

Internationally, the winner of the 2024 election will shape America's role in global affairs. Trump's "America First" doctrine emphasizes nationalism, reduced commitments abroad, and renegotiated alliances to prioritize American interests. Harris, however, favors strengthening alliances and recommitting to global agreements on climate and human rights. The 2024 election could shift international relationships, affecting trade policies, climate agreements, and alliances that have defined the post-WWII world order.

Analyzing the Contenders: Donald Trump and Kamala Harris

Donald Trump

Donald Trump, former president and business mogul, remains one of the most polarizing figures in American politics. Known for his unconventional style and unfiltered rhetoric, Trump has built a strong base among voters who see him as a political outsider willing to "drain the swamp" and challenge entrenched interests. His policies are rooted in economic nationalism, immigration control, and deregulation, which he argues will bring jobs back to American soil and protect national interests. Despite facing multiple controversies, including investigations and impeachment trials, Trump's support has endured among his core base, who view him as a defender of American identity and sovereignty.

Trump's appeal lies in his ability to tap into the frustrations of working-class Americans who feel alienated by globalization and cultural changes. His 2024 campaign aims to rekindle the sense of national pride that characterized his previous term, focusing on a return to "law and order," border security, and policies that prioritize American workers.

However, his critics argue that Trump's policies contribute to division and that his administration's approach undermines democratic norms and institutions. His stance on climate change, immigration, and international alliances have sparked significant debate, making him a figure of both admiration and alarm.

Kamala Harris

Vice President Kamala Harris brings a groundbreaking presence to the 2024 election. As a former California attorney general and senator, Harris has a career that reflects her commitment to justice reform, healthcare expansion, and progressive policies. Her campaign embodies the ideals of inclusivity, social equity, and a more active federal government role in addressing systemic challenges.

Harris' supporters believe she offers a much-needed progressive vision to tackle urgent issues like racial injustice, climate change, and healthcare access. Her candidacy is historic, as she is the first woman of color on a major party's presidential ticket, symbolizing a shift towards a more diverse and representative America.

Harris' policy positions include a strong focus on climate action, expanding healthcare through public options, and reforms in criminal justice. She also emphasizes the importance of America's global leadership, advocating for renewed commitments to alliances and international organizations.

Critics, however, argue that her policies may lead to increased government spending and intervention in private industries, raising concerns among fiscal conservatives. Nevertheless, Harris is a compelling figure for those seeking change, particularly among younger, more progressive voters who view her as a candidate poised to lead America towards a more equitable future.

In sum, the 2024 election is not just a contest between two candidates but a referendum on America's path forward. Trump and Harris stand as symbols of two distinct visions: one that seeks to preserve traditional values and prioritize national sovereignty, and another that envisions a more inclusive, globally connected, and environmentally responsible America.

Each represents contrasting answers to the pressing questions that face the country: How will America approach economic recovery, climate change, social justice, and its role in the world? As voters prepare to make their choice, the significance of this election cannot be overstated—it will set the direction of American policy, values, and identity for years to come.

AMERICA DECIDES *2024*

CHAPTER ONE

The Historical Landscape of U.S. Presidential Elections

The history of U.S. presidential elections reveals an ongoing evolution in the nation's partisan landscape, shaped by shifting social, economic, and ideological forces. The early years of the American Republic were marked by a relatively small number of political factions, largely divided between the Federalists and the Democratic-Republicans.

This era saw debates over the balance of federal and state power, the structure of government, and foreign alliances, as the fledgling nation sought to establish itself. The Federalists, led by figures like

Alexander Hamilton, advocated for a strong centralized government and policies favoring industrial development, while the Democratic-Republicans, led by Thomas Jefferson and James Madison, favored agrarianism and a limited federal role.

By the mid-19th century, these initial divides gave way to more polarized factions as new social and economic issues, particularly slavery, defined the political landscape. The collapse of the Whig Party in the 1850s and the rise of the Republican Party, founded on anti-slavery principles, set the stage for a deeply polarized era that culminated in the Civil War.

The Republican Party emerged as the dominant party of the North, advocating for the abolition of slavery and a more expansive federal government, while the Democratic Party became aligned with Southern interests. This period, known as the Third Party System, was marked by intense partisan loyalty, with elections serving as referenda on issues like Reconstruction, civil rights, and economic modernization.

The 20th century brought further realignment, particularly during the Great Depression and the New Deal. Franklin D. Roosevelt's New Deal coalition united working-class voters, African Americans, and other marginalized groups under the Democratic banner, transforming the party into an advocate for government intervention in the economy. Meanwhile, the Republicans became more associated with limited government and fiscal conservatism.

This alignment persisted for much of the 20th century, although it saw notable shifts in the 1960s and 1970s, as civil rights, the Vietnam War, and social issues like abortion and women's rights began to reshape party identities. By the 1980s, the Republican Party, under Ronald Reagan, became the standard-bearer for a conservative agenda that emphasized limited government, lower taxes, and a strong military, while the Democrats positioned themselves as advocates for social programs, civil rights, and labor rights.

The current partisan divide, often traced back to the 1990s, has deepened due to factors like media polarization, economic inequality, and the rise of identity politics. Issues once seen as common ground have become ideological battlegrounds, with debates over immigration, healthcare, and environmental policy reflecting broader philosophical differences. Today, the polarization between Democrats and Republicans is more pronounced than ever, shaping not only policy outcomes but also the very fabric of American political discourse.

Key Elections That Defined America's Path

Throughout U.S. history, certain presidential elections have served as turning points, fundamentally altering the nation's trajectory and reshaping its political and social landscape.

- 1800: Jefferson vs. Adams

The election of 1800 was a pivotal moment in American politics, marking the first peaceful transfer of power between two parties. Thomas Jefferson's victory over incumbent John Adams represented a shift towards a more democratic ethos, challenging the Federalist emphasis on centralized power.

Known as the "Revolution of 1800," Jefferson's election laid the groundwork for a government more responsive to the common citizen and less inclined toward elitist rule. This election also introduced enduring themes in American politics, including the role of partisanship and the importance of civic engagement.

- 1860: Lincoln vs. Breckinridge/Douglas/Bell

The election of Abraham Lincoln in 1860 was a defining moment in American history, triggering the secession of Southern states and leading to the Civil War. Lincoln's anti-slavery platform, which emphasized the containment of slavery rather than its immediate abolition, was a catalyst for Southern states fearing the end of their social and economic order.

This election underscored the profound regional divisions in the U.S. and highlighted the power of the presidency to steer the country through existential crises. The election of 1860 reshaped the Union and set the stage for Reconstruction, the end of slavery, and the expansion of federal authority.

- 1932: FDR vs. Hoover

Franklin D. Roosevelt's victory over Herbert Hoover in 1932 marked the beginning of the New Deal era and a realignment of American politics. In response to the Great Depression, Roosevelt implemented unprecedented federal intervention in the economy, fundamentally altering the relationship between the government and the American people.

The New Deal coalition brought together a diverse range of voters—including urban workers, farmers, African Americans, and intellectuals—creating a Democratic majority that would dominate U.S. politics for decades. The election of 1932 remains a key moment in the development of modern American liberalism and the social safety net.

- 1980: Reagan vs. Carter

The election of Ronald Reagan in 1980 signaled a conservative revolution, ushering in an era of free-market policies, deregulation, and a reassertion of American military power. Reagan's victory over Jimmy Carter reflected a backlash against the perceived failures of liberal policies and the social upheavals of the 1960s and 1970s.

Reagan's presidency would shape conservative ideology for decades, influencing the Republican Party's emphasis on tax cuts, small government, and a strong national defense. The 1980 election also highlighted the power of media and communication in modern campaigning, as Reagan's charisma and optimism resonated deeply with the electorate.

- 2008: Obama vs. McCain

The election of Barack Obama in 2008 was a historic moment in American history, marking the first time an African American was elected president. Obama's campaign centered on themes of hope, change, and unity, appealing to a country weary from economic turmoil and divisive politics.

His election reflected shifts in the American electorate, including the rising influence of younger voters and minorities. Obama's presidency addressed issues like healthcare reform, economic recovery, and foreign policy in a globalized world, while also highlighting deep divisions in the country regarding race, healthcare, and government intervention.

A Review of Election Narratives: Myths and Realities

U.S. presidential elections are often surrounded by narratives that can shape public perception but don't always align with historical realities. These myths are frequently used to simplify complex dynamics or reinforce particular viewpoints, influencing how people understand the outcomes and significance of each election.

One of the most enduring myths is the idea that American elections are always a "mandate" from the people. In reality, many presidential elections have been won by narrow margins or through the electoral college rather than a popular vote majority.

Presidents elected under such circumstances often face challenges in governing due to a divided electorate, undermining the notion that their victories reflect an overwhelming endorsement of their platform. This reality has become more pronounced in recent years, as electoral college results have diverged from the popular vote in multiple elections.

Another common narrative is that certain elections represent a complete ideological shift. While it's true that elections like 1932 and 1980 ushered in significant changes, American politics is often more cyclical than linear. Policy reversals are common, and shifts in one direction are frequently countered by moves in the opposite direction in subsequent years. This cyclical nature is evident in the oscillation between liberal and conservative policies, reflecting an electorate that often favors moderation over extremes.

A third myth is the belief that presidential campaigns are solely decided on policy issues. In reality, factors like candidate charisma, media portrayal, and unforeseen events (such as economic crises or international conflicts) play a significant role in election outcomes.

The 1960 election, for example, highlighted the importance of televised debates, with John F. Kennedy's telegenic presence helping to sway public opinion against Richard Nixon. Similarly, the 2008 election was influenced by the financial crisis, which underscored the need for economic reform and worked to the advantage of Barack Obama's campaign message of hope and change.

Understanding these myths and realities offers valuable insight into the factors that truly shape presidential elections. While policy is undoubtedly a factor, the context, personalities, and unforeseen events often

*AMERICA DECIDES *2024**

play an equally, if not more, decisive role. Each election is shaped by unique circumstances and offers a snapshot of the nation's priorities, fears, and aspirations at a particular moment in time.

CHAPTER TWO

The Candidates - Backgrounds, Visions, and Leadership Styles

Donald Trump, the 45th President of the United States, has been a defining and divisive figure in American politics. Coming from a business background as a real estate mogul and reality television personality, Trump's initial entry into politics was unconventional.

His 2016 campaign, based on his "Make America Great Again" slogan, appealed to a wide spectrum of voters who felt disillusioned with traditional politicians and the political establishment. For many of his supporters, Trump was seen as a bold outsider, someone who would "drain the swamp" and challenge long-standing norms within Washington, D.C.

As president, Trump's policies were marked by his commitment to an "America First" agenda, with a focus on economic nationalism, border security, and deregulatory initiatives. His administration implemented tax cuts, pursued a trade war with China, and placed heavy emphasis on reshaping immigration policies.

Trump also focused on rolling back environmental regulations, arguing that such policies hindered economic growth and energy independence. His leadership style was characterized by direct, often confrontational communication and a preference for making announcements on social media, bypassing traditional channels of political discourse.

Trump's presidency was frequently marred by controversy, from his handling of racial justice protests to his management of the COVID-19 pandemic, and his communication style often amplified these divisions. His approach to the media was particularly combative, frequently labeling it as the "enemy of the people," which further fueled distrust among his supporters.

However, his base remained steadfast, seeing his brashness as a refreshing alternative to what they viewed as politically correct and scripted leadership. His appeal lay in his ability to speak to a sense of nostalgia, particularly among those who felt left behind by the rapid social and economic changes of recent decades.

After leaving office, Trump's influence in the Republican Party only grew, as he endorsed candidates who aligned with his vision and criticized those he deemed insufficiently loyal. His 2024 campaign picks up where his 2020 platform left off, once again focusing on issues like border security, economic independence, and "law and order." For his supporters, Trump remains a champion of American sovereignty and values. For his critics, however, he symbolizes a threat to democratic institutions and norms, as well as a leader who often stokes division rather than unity.

Kamala Harris: Firsts, Fights, and Futures

Kamala Harris, the current Vice President of the United States, is a historic figure in American politics. She is the first female, Black, and South Asian vice president, making her candidacy in 2024 both symbolically and politically significant. Harris' career in public service began in California, where she served as district attorney of San Francisco and later as the state's attorney general.

In these roles, Harris built a reputation as a tough prosecutor, focusing on issues like child exploitation and housing fraud, but also received criticism for her approach to criminal justice, with some arguing that her policies disproportionately affected marginalized communities.

In 2016, Harris was elected to the U.S. Senate, where she became known for her sharp questioning during committee hearings, especially in the confirmation hearings of Trump administration officials. Her platform in the Senate focused on issues such as healthcare reform, climate change, and criminal justice reform.

Harris' policy proposals often reflect a progressive vision, advocating for expanded social services, climate action, and economic equity. As vice president, she has worked closely on issues like immigration reform, leading efforts to address the root causes of migration from Central America, and

COVID-19 vaccination efforts, particularly in underserved communities.

Harris' leadership style emphasizes empathy, coalition-building, and inclusivity, which she views as essential for addressing the diverse needs of the American public. Her 2024 campaign is likely to reflect these themes, positioning her as a leader committed to tackling systemic inequalities and building a more inclusive future.

For many voters, Harris represents the future of the Democratic Party, one that embraces diversity and progressive values. Her background as a daughter of immigrants and a woman of color adds depth to her candidacy, symbolizing a shift towards a more representative and inclusive America.

However, Harris also faces significant challenges. Critics argue that her policy stances are too liberal for moderate and independent voters, and her relatively short tenure as vice president has led to scrutiny over her lack of extensive executive experience. Additionally, her prosecutorial background has come under renewed examination by both progressive and conservative factions, who question her record on criminal justice issues.

Nonetheless, Harris' supporters see her as a transformative leader, capable of guiding America toward a more equitable society and reclaiming America's standing on the global stage.

Contrasting Leadership Philosophies and Styles

The 2024 election offers voters a clear choice between two vastly different leadership philosophies embodied by Donald Trump and Kamala Harris. These contrasting approaches reflect not only their personal experiences and beliefs but also the divergent values and priorities of the constituencies they represent.

Trump's Approach: Strength, Nationalism, and Directness

Trump's leadership style can be described as populist and direct, characterized by a strong emphasis on national sovereignty and economic protectionism. He often prioritizes immediate, tangible results over long-term strategic planning, a trait rooted in his background as a businessman. His presidency showcased his penchant for cutting through bureaucracy to achieve goals, evident in his rapid deregulation policies and tax reform efforts. Trump's leadership is also marked by his preference for strong, centralized executive power, often viewing the checks and balances of the American system as obstacles to progress.

His approach to foreign policy is grounded in the "America First" doctrine, which prioritizes national interests over international cooperation. This philosophy often leads to unilateral actions or renegotiated agreements, as seen in his approach to NATO, trade agreements, and alliances with other countries. Trump's communication style is equally direct, frequently using social media to bypass traditional media and deliver his message directly to his base. This unfiltered style resonates with supporters who see him as authentic and unafraid to speak his mind, but it alienates critics who view his rhetoric as inflammatory and divisive.

Harris' Approach: Inclusivity, Diplomacy, and Long-Term Reform

In contrast, Harris' leadership philosophy centers on inclusivity, coalition-building, and progressive reform. She advocates for policies that seek to address systemic inequalities, whether in healthcare, education, or criminal justice. Harris' background as a prosecutor and legislator has shaped her view of governance as a collaborative effort that requires building coalitions and engaging with a broad range of stakeholders. Her style tends to be more measured and diplomatic, seeking to address issues from multiple perspectives and building consensus among diverse groups.

Harris' approach to foreign policy emphasizes multilateralism and the importance of America's role as a global leader on issues like climate change and human rights. She believes in strengthening alliances and re-engaging with international organizations to address global challenges collaboratively. This contrasts sharply with

Trump's preference for unilateralism and economic nationalism.

Harris' communication style is also more traditional, favoring carefully crafted public addresses and policy-driven discourse over spontaneous social media posts. Her supporters view her as a steady, empathetic leader who can bring people together to solve complex issues, but her critics argue that her style may lack the decisiveness needed to address urgent crises swiftly.

Policy Priorities and Vision for America

At the core of their contrasting leadership philosophies are fundamentally different visions for America. Trump's vision is one of a resurgent, self-reliant America that prioritizes its citizens over global entanglements. His focus on issues like border security, trade protectionism, and deregulation reflects a belief in the power of American independence and strength. His administration's policies reflect this worldview, aiming to protect American jobs, strengthen national borders, and limit government intervention in business.

Harris' vision, on the other hand, is rooted in a progressive agenda that seeks to build a more inclusive society. Her focus on social justice, climate action, and healthcare reform reflects a commitment to addressing systemic issues and expanding opportunities for all Americans. Her policy priorities aim to create a more equitable society, with targeted initiatives for marginalized communities and policies that reflect the evolving demographics of the country. Harris' supporters see her as a leader for a changing America, one that is diverse, interconnected, and ready to confront global challenges.

Overall, in the 2024 election, voters are faced with two starkly different leadership styles and visions for America's future. Trump's approach is characterized by a brash confidence and a commitment to protecting national interests, resonating with those who prioritize strength and self-sufficiency. Harris, on the other hand, represents a more progressive, inclusive, and globally-minded approach, appealing to those who believe in a collaborative path forward.

This contrast highlights the broader ideological divide in the United States, offering voters a choice between two distinct paths: one that seeks to preserve and protect traditional American values, and another that envisions a forward-thinking, inclusive America ready to tackle the challenges of a globalized world. This choice will not only shape the next four years but will have lasting implications for the nation's identity, values, and role in the world.

CHAPTER THREE

The Economy - Competing Plans for Prosperity

Donald Trump's approach to the economy is grounded in a conservative, free-market ideology aimed at deregulation, tax cuts, and a strong focus on national interests over international agreements. His economic agenda, widely known as "America First," advocates for policies that, in his view, prioritize American workers, businesses, and the broader national economy.

This strategy reflects Trump's belief that reducing government intervention, boosting manufacturing, and promoting self-reliance are essential for sustainable economic growth.

*AMERICA DECIDES *2024**

During his first term, Trump implemented the Tax Cuts and Jobs Act (TCJA) of 2017, which significantly reduced corporate tax rates from 35% to 21% and provided tax cuts for individuals, particularly those in higher income brackets. His administration argued that lowering corporate taxes would encourage investment, lead to job creation, and boost overall economic growth. While the cuts did stimulate some business investments, they also led to a substantial increase in the federal deficit.

Critics argued that the tax cuts disproportionately benefited corporations and the wealthy, with limited impact on middle- and lower-income families, who faced only temporary tax reductions compared to the permanent cuts for businesses.

Another cornerstone of Trump's economic policy was a strong stance on trade. He argued that previous administrations had allowed unfair trade practices, especially with China, to harm American jobs and industries. In response, Trump imposed tariffs on Chinese imports, initiating a trade war that led to tariffs on a wide range of products.

His administration also renegotiated the North American Free Trade Agreement (NAFTA), replacing it with the United States-Mexico-Canada Agreement (USMCA). Supporters argued that these measures helped protect American jobs and industries, particularly in manufacturing and agriculture, though critics contended that tariffs ultimately raised costs for American consumers and created challenges for industries reliant on foreign materials.

Trump's policies on deregulation were another key component of his economic playbook. His administration rolled back numerous regulations across sectors, including environmental protections, banking oversight, and labor standards. Trump argued that deregulation would encourage business growth by reducing the burden of government requirements.

However, opponents claimed that deregulation came at a cost, particularly to environmental protections and worker safety. For instance, loosening restrictions on emissions and energy production was seen as a win for the fossil fuel industry but raised concerns about climate change and environmental degradation.

One of the biggest challenges to Trump's economic strategy is the sustainability of his approach, especially as critics argue that tax cuts and deregulation might not have the long-term impact needed to benefit the broader economy. His strategy also faced a major test with the COVID-19 pandemic, which led to unprecedented unemployment levels and economic instability. Trump's response focused on quick reopening measures and stimulus payments, aiming to boost spending and get people back to work.

However, this approach received mixed reactions, with some arguing that the rapid push to reopen contributed to prolonged economic and health challenges. In 2024, Trump's campaign is likely to emphasize a return to his core principles, promising a "revitalized" economy based on reduced taxes, strong borders, and trade policies aimed at favoring American workers.

Harris' Vision for Economic Reform and Inclusion

Kamala Harris' economic vision presents a sharp contrast to Trump's "America First" approach. Her economic platform is rooted in a progressive vision that seeks to address income inequality, expand social safety nets, and invest in sustainable industries that align with environmental goals.

As vice president, Harris worked closely with the Biden administration to support initiatives that emphasized inclusive growth, such as the expansion of the Child Tax Credit, student debt relief, and climate-focused investments through the Inflation Reduction Act. Her 2024 economic agenda builds on these efforts, aiming to create a fairer and more resilient economy.

A central component of Harris' economic policy is wealth redistribution and income equity. She has proposed higher taxes on the wealthiest Americans and corporations, arguing that the wealth gap between the rich and poor is unsustainable and harmful to the broader economy. Harris' tax policy includes rolling back parts of the Trump tax cuts, specifically targeting high-income earners and corporations to fund social programs and infrastructure projects.

Supporters believe that this approach would help to address income inequality and provide more funding for essential services, while opponents worry that higher taxes could discourage investment and economic growth.

Harris is also an advocate for expanding social programs, which she believes are essential for creating an inclusive economy. Her platform includes expanding access to healthcare, increasing affordable housing, and investing in education, especially in underserved communities. The goal, Harris argues, is to create an economy where more people have the tools and resources needed to achieve financial stability.

This includes a commitment to universal pre-K, tuition-free community college, and more affordable childcare options, which she sees as crucial for supporting working families and enabling broader workforce participation.

Climate change and sustainable energy development are key aspects of Harris' economic strategy. She envisions a "green economy" that not only addresses the environmental crisis but also creates new job opportunities in sectors like renewable energy, electric vehicles, and infrastructure modernization.

Harris supports investments in green technology and sustainable practices as a way to both stimulate economic growth and ensure long-term resilience. She argues that climate action is not only necessary for the environment but also offers an economic opportunity, particularly in high-demand fields like solar and wind energy.

To address the changing nature of the workforce, Harris has proposed job training and reskilling programs aimed at preparing Americans for new industries. Recognizing that automation and globalization have shifted the job market, she emphasizes the need for government-supported initiatives to help workers transition into growing sectors.

Additionally, Harris' platform supports union rights and labor protections, which she believes are essential for ensuring fair wages and workplace conditions. Her approach to the economy is centered on the belief that when more people have access to good jobs and economic opportunities, the entire country benefits.

Economic Theories and Realities: Who Has the Stronger Plan?

In evaluating the economic visions of Donald Trump and Kamala Harris, it becomes clear that each candidate's approach is rooted in distinct economic theories and priorities. Trump's economic strategy aligns with a conservative, supply-side perspective, while Harris' platform is more aligned with progressive

Keynesian principles focused on income redistribution and government intervention.

Trump's Supply-Side Approach

Supply-side economics, which emphasizes tax cuts and deregulation as a means to stimulate production and growth, is central to Trump's approach. This theory suggests that reducing taxes on businesses and individuals, especially high earners, leads to increased investment and economic expansion, with benefits eventually "trickling down" to all levels of society. Trump's tax cuts and deregulation efforts reflect this philosophy, aiming to create an environment in which businesses can thrive with minimal government interference.

Critics of supply-side economics, however, argue that the benefits of tax cuts often do not reach lower-income individuals. Studies on the effects of Trump's tax cuts indicate that while some corporations and wealthy individuals saw significant financial benefits, the impact on wages and job creation was less pronounced than anticipated.

This criticism suggests that supply-side policies might be more beneficial to shareholders and executives than to everyday workers. Moreover, supply-side economics often relies on the assumption that economic growth will offset revenue losses from tax cuts, a notion that has been challenged by the rising federal deficit in recent years.

Harris' Progressive Keynesian Approach

Harris' economic strategy is rooted in Keynesian principles, which emphasize government intervention in the economy to promote growth and reduce inequality. Her approach involves a combination of higher taxes on the wealthy, increased public spending on social programs, and targeted investments in sectors like renewable energy and infrastructure. Proponents of this approach argue that it can stimulate demand by putting more money in the hands of middle- and lower-income individuals, who are more likely to spend it, thereby boosting the economy.

Keynesian economics suggests that government spending can act as a counterbalance during economic downturns and help address structural inequalities. By investing in education, healthcare, and green infrastructure, Harris aims to create a more equitable and sustainable economic future. However, critics of this approach argue that higher taxes and increased government intervention could stifle economic growth and place a burden on businesses, potentially leading to slower job creation and reduced private investment.

Evaluating the Realities and Potential Outcomes

Both Trump and Harris' economic plans have their advantages and limitations, and the ultimate impact of each approach would depend on external factors, including global economic conditions and domestic policy implementation.

Trump's focus on tax cuts and deregulation could lead to short-term economic growth, especially for large businesses and high-income earners, but the long-term sustainability of this approach is uncertain. Critics argue that his policies could increase the federal deficit and exacerbate income inequality, potentially leading to economic instability. Moreover, Trump's stance on trade and tariffs could create short-term gains for certain industries but risk damaging international relationships and increasing costs for American consumers.

Harris' approach, on the other hand, emphasizes long-term investment in social programs and sustainable industries, which could foster a more resilient and equitable economy. Her emphasis on climate action and green technology could position the U.S. as a global leader in sustainable development, but it would require significant initial investment. Opponents caution that higher taxes and increased government spending could slow economic growth and discourage private investment, though Harris argues that the benefits of a more inclusive economy would outweigh these concerns.

Overall, in the 2024 election, voters face a critical choice between two competing economic visions. Trump's strategy appeals to those who believe in minimal government intervention, lower taxes, and a strong focus on American sovereignty in trade. Harris' vision, meanwhile, seeks to address inequality, invest in sustainable industries, and strengthen social programs to build a more inclusive economy.

The outcome of this debate will shape the direction of the U.S. economy, determining not only how wealth is distributed but also how prepared the nation will be to confront future economic and environmental challenges.

CHAPTER FOUR

Healthcare in America - Access, Affordability, and Policy Proposals

The Affordable Care Act (ACA), enacted in 2010 during President Obama's administration, was a landmark piece of legislation aimed at overhauling the American healthcare system. It introduced significant changes, most notably expanding health insurance coverage, mandating protections for people with pre-existing conditions, and establishing marketplaces where individuals could purchase subsidized health insurance.

The ACA also expanded Medicaid in many states, extending coverage to millions of low-income Americans who had previously lacked access to healthcare.

The ACA's primary goals were to make healthcare more affordable, improve the quality of care, and increase coverage across all demographics. By creating a mandate for insurance and offering government subsidies, the ACA intended to broaden access and make healthcare a right rather than a privilege. Through provisions like the Essential Health Benefits package, the ACA also sought to ensure that all insurance plans covered basic healthcare needs, including emergency services, maternity care, and preventive care.

However, the ACA has faced substantial criticism and legal challenges since its inception. Critics argue that the individual mandate, which required all Americans to purchase health insurance or face a penalty, was an overreach of federal authority. Opponents also claim that the ACA contributed to increased healthcare premiums for some Americans, particularly those who did not qualify for subsidies.

Despite the intentions behind the law, the issue of rising costs remained a point of contention. Moreover, some states chose not to expand Medicaid, leaving gaps in coverage for low-income individuals in those regions.

The ACA also spurred debates about the role of government in healthcare. Supporters view it as a foundational step toward universal healthcare, while opponents argue that it increased government interference in the healthcare industry. In 2017, the individual mandate was effectively eliminated when Congress passed a tax reform bill setting the penalty for not having insurance to zero. This move sparked discussions about the ACA's long-term viability, as the individual mandate was initially seen as crucial to ensuring a balanced insurance pool.

Despite its challenges, the ACA has left an enduring legacy on the U.S. healthcare system. As of 2024, millions of Americans rely on ACA-subsidized plans, and protections for pre-existing conditions remain highly popular. The ACA remains a central issue in American politics, symbolizing the ongoing debate between advocates of expanded government intervention in healthcare and those who favor a more market-driven approach.

For voters in the 2024 election, the future of the ACA—and healthcare reform more broadly—remains a top concern, as both candidates have offered differing perspectives on how to address the system's ongoing issues.

Trump's Approach to Healthcare and Reform

Donald Trump's approach to healthcare has been shaped by his administration's criticism of the ACA and its commitment to repealing and replacing it. Throughout his presidency, Trump argued that the ACA was flawed, pointing to rising premiums, limited provider options, and what he perceived as excessive federal control over healthcare. His administration repeatedly attempted to dismantle the ACA, supporting lawsuits and legislative efforts aimed at weakening or eliminating key components of the law. However, despite repeated efforts, a comprehensive repeal was never achieved, and the ACA remains largely intact.

During his presidency, Trump's healthcare agenda centered on promoting free-market principles, reducing costs through deregulation, and offering alternatives to the ACA. One of his administration's significant policy moves was expanding access to short-term health insurance plans. These plans, which do not have to meet the ACA's coverage requirements, are often cheaper but typically provide fewer benefits.

Supporters argue that short-term plans offer a more affordable alternative for individuals who may not need comprehensive coverage, while critics contend that these plans undermine the ACA's standards and leave policyholders vulnerable to unexpected healthcare expenses.

Another major aspect of Trump's healthcare strategy was to support high-risk pools and health savings accounts (HSAs). High-risk pools were proposed as a way to cover individuals with pre-existing conditions outside the standard insurance market. Trump argued that this would stabilize the insurance market by separating high-cost patients from the general pool, thereby lowering premiums.

HSAs were promoted as a means to give individuals more control over their healthcare spending, with tax-free savings that could be used for medical expenses. However, critics of this approach argue that high-risk pools are underfunded and often provide inadequate coverage, while HSAs primarily benefit higher-income individuals who can afford to set aside money for medical expenses.

Trump's healthcare policy also included efforts to increase transparency in pricing, aiming to empower consumers to make more informed choices about their healthcare. In 2019, his administration finalized a rule requiring hospitals to disclose prices for procedures, an initiative intended to foster competition and drive down costs. While this transparency rule was met with approval by some consumer advocacy groups, critics argued that price disclosure alone does not address the underlying issues of healthcare affordability.

As Trump re-enters the political arena in 2024, he has reiterated his commitment to a healthcare system based on choice, competition, and individual responsibility. His platform continues to emphasize alternatives to the ACA, advocating for market-driven solutions that he argues will reduce costs and improve access. Trump's stance resonates with voters who are skeptical of government-led healthcare solutions, but it also faces criticism from those who believe that such approaches fail to address the root causes of the healthcare crisis in America.

Harris' Plans for Expanding and Reinventing Healthcare

Kamala Harris' healthcare vision builds on the ACA's foundation and emphasizes expanding access, improving affordability, and addressing inequalities within the healthcare system. Harris has long advocated for a stronger government role in healthcare, and her 2024 platform reflects a commitment to advancing universal access while ensuring quality care and addressing the unique needs of marginalized communities.

As vice president, Harris supported policies like expanding the ACA, lowering prescription drug costs, and increasing funding for mental health services. In her 2024 campaign, she seeks to further these efforts with bold reforms aimed at creating a more inclusive healthcare system.

A key component of Harris' healthcare plan is the establishment of a public option—a government-run health insurance plan that would be available alongside private insurance options. Unlike a single-payer system, which would eliminate private insurance, the public option would coexist with private plans, giving Americans a choice.

Harris believes that this approach can drive down costs by introducing competition and giving consumers an affordable alternative to private insurance. The public option is designed to ensure that no one is uninsured while preserving individual choice, a position that she argues strikes a balance between universal access and personal freedom.

In addition to the public option, Harris is committed to lowering prescription drug costs, an issue that has become a significant financial burden for many Americans. Her plan includes allowing Medicare to negotiate drug prices directly with pharmaceutical companies, a policy that proponents argue could lead to substantial savings for both the government and consumers.

Harris also supports capping out-of-pocket expenses for prescription drugs and making generic medications more accessible. She argues that reducing drug prices is not only a matter of affordability but also a matter of health equity, as high costs often prevent vulnerable populations from accessing the medications they need.

Another critical element of Harris' healthcare platform is addressing health disparities. Harris has emphasized the importance of tackling systemic inequalities in healthcare access, which disproportionately affect communities of color, rural populations, and low-income individuals.

Her approach includes increasing funding for community health centers, expanding telemedicine services, and enhancing Medicaid funding to ensure that underserved areas receive adequate care. Harris has also advocated for maternal health reforms, particularly to address the high rates of maternal mortality among Black women.

Her healthcare strategy underscores the belief that healthcare should be a right, not a privilege, and that the system must work for all Americans, regardless of income, location, or background.

Mental health and substance abuse treatment are also focal points of Harris' healthcare plan. She advocates for expanding mental health coverage under the ACA and increasing federal funding for mental health services. Harris believes that mental health care should be integrated into primary care settings to reduce stigma and make treatment more accessible. Her platform also calls for enhanced support for individuals struggling with addiction, including expanded access to treatment programs and recovery resources.

In sum, Harris' healthcare vision reflects a commitment to equity, access, and affordability. She argues that a public option, combined with targeted reforms on drug pricing, health disparities, and mental health, can create a healthcare system that serves all Americans. Her approach contrasts with Trump's, as she favors a more significant government role in regulating and providing healthcare, believing that this is necessary to address systemic issues within the current system.

The healthcare debate in the 2024 election reflects two distinct philosophies regarding the role of government, access to care, and the importance of affordability. Trump's approach leans toward market-driven solutions and individual choice, emphasizing transparency, deregulation, and the expansion of private alternatives to the ACA.

His proposals resonate with voters who prefer limited government intervention and view the ACA as an overreach that restricts consumer choice. Trump's healthcare platform seeks to empower individuals to make their own healthcare decisions and reduce reliance on government programs.

On the other hand, Harris' vision builds on the ACA and moves toward expanded access through a public option and stronger government involvement. Her proposals emphasize health equity, aiming to reduce disparities and ensure that all Americans can access quality care regardless of income. Harris' healthcare platform reflects a belief that a more inclusive system will create a healthier and more equitable society. For her supporters, healthcare is seen as a fundamental right, requiring government intervention to address structural inequalities and high costs.

In this election, voters are presented with a clear choice on healthcare. Trump's market-focused strategy prioritizes freedom from government intervention, while Harris' plan envisions a government-supported framework that addresses affordability, access, and systemic disparities. The outcome of this debate will have profound implications for millions of Americans, shaping not only healthcare policy but also the nation's broader understanding of the role of government in ensuring the well-being of its citizens.

CHAPTER FIVE

Immigration and Border Policies - Balancing Security and Humanity

Immigration has been one of the most defining and polarizing issues of Donald Trump's political career. His stance on immigration, characterized by a strict emphasis on border security and immigration enforcement, gained widespread attention through his "Build the Wall" slogan during the 2016 campaign.

For Trump, building a physical barrier along the U.S.-Mexico border was not only a practical solution to illegal immigration but also a symbol of his administration's commitment to national security, sovereignty, and law enforcement. By advocating for the wall, Trump sought to address issues such as illegal immigration, drug trafficking, and human smuggling, which he argued posed significant risks to American communities.

During his presidency, Trump's administration diverted billions of dollars to construct portions of the border wall, despite resistance from Congress. By 2020, his administration had built over 450 miles of new or replacement barriers, though critics pointed out that much of the construction was reinforcement of existing barriers rather than entirely new wall segments.

This initiative, while praised by his supporters as a concrete step toward border security, was controversial, both financially and morally. Critics argued that the wall was an ineffective and expensive solution, failing to address the root causes of immigration while also damaging the environment and disrupting communities along the border.

Beyond the wall, Trump's approach to immigration included aggressive enforcement policies aimed at reducing illegal immigration and restricting asylum. His administration implemented a "zero tolerance" policy, leading to the separation of thousands of families at the border—a move that sparked national outrage and became one of the administration's most contentious issues.

Trump defended the policy as necessary for enforcing immigration laws, while opponents argued that it was inhumane and traumatizing to children and families fleeing violence and poverty. The administration also restricted asylum applications through the Migrant Protection Protocols, known as the "Remain in Mexico" policy, requiring asylum seekers to wait in Mexico while their cases were processed in U.S. courts.

In addition, Trump implemented significant restrictions on legal immigration, arguing that a lower influx of immigrants would benefit American workers by reducing competition in the labor market. His administration introduced measures such as the "public charge" rule, which restricted green card eligibility for immigrants who might rely on public assistance.

The administration also implemented a temporary ban on immigration during the COVID-19 pandemic, citing health and economic concerns. These policies drew criticism for being overly harsh and discriminatory, with opponents arguing that they perpetuated negative stereotypes and disregarded the contributions of immigrants to American society and the economy.

Despite the controversies, Trump's immigration policies resonated with his base, particularly those who felt that previous administrations had neglected border security and the enforcement of immigration laws. For his supporters,

Trump's stance on immigration symbolized his commitment to American sovereignty and his willingness to challenge political correctness on a divisive issue.

In the 2024 election, Trump's immigration platform remains focused on continuing his efforts to "finish the wall," increase deportations of undocumented immigrants, and impose stricter vetting procedures. His stance reflects a belief that stringent immigration policies are essential to maintaining national security, protecting American jobs, and preserving American culture.

Harris' Approach to Immigration Reform

In contrast to Trump's hardline approach, Kamala Harris has championed a more humane and inclusive perspective on immigration reform. Her platform emphasizes compassion, fairness, and the need for a comprehensive immigration policy that respects human rights while addressing security concerns.

Harris argues that America's strength lies in its diversity, and her approach to immigration reflects a belief that the country should embrace its role as a destination for those seeking opportunity and refuge. She views immigrants as an integral part of the American fabric and has advocated for policies that promote family unity, expand legal pathways to citizenship, and address the root causes of migration.

As vice president, Harris took a prominent role in addressing the factors that drive migration from Central America, working to develop strategies to reduce poverty, violence, and corruption in countries like Guatemala, Honduras, and El Salvador.

Her efforts included securing commitments from American businesses to invest in the region and providing U.S. aid to improve economic conditions, healthcare, and education. Harris argues that by addressing the root causes of migration, the U.S. can reduce the number of people compelled to flee their home countries, thereby easing the strain on the border.

Harris' platform includes a pathway to citizenship for the millions of undocumented immigrants already residing in the U.S., particularly those who were brought to the country as children, known as Dreamers. The Deferred Action for Childhood Arrivals (DACA) program, which allows Dreamers to live and work in the U.S. without fear of deportation, has been a cornerstone of her immigration vision.

Harris advocates for making DACA protections permanent and providing Dreamers with a clear path to citizenship, arguing that these individuals are already contributing to society and deserve the opportunity to fully integrate as American citizens.

Another key element of Harris' immigration policy is her commitment to reforming the asylum process to make it more humane and efficient. She has criticized Trump's policies, such as family separation and the "Remain in Mexico" program, which she views as punitive and inconsistent with American values.

Harris proposes increasing the resources allocated to immigration courts, allowing for quicker processing of asylum claims and reducing the backlog of cases. She also supports expanding humanitarian protections for vulnerable groups, such as those fleeing domestic violence or persecution due to gender identity, which she argues aligns with international human rights standards.

Harris has also addressed the need for border security, though her approach focuses more on modernizing border technology and improving immigration infrastructure than on physical barriers. She supports investing in surveillance technology, such as drones and sensors, to enhance border security without disrupting communities or ecosystems. Harris contends that a balanced approach to border security can protect national interests while respecting the rights of immigrants and maintaining America's reputation as a nation of refuge.

In sum, Harris' immigration vision emphasizes a compassionate and pragmatic approach, aiming to balance security with humanity. Her stance contrasts sharply with

Trump's, as she focuses on creating legal pathways to citizenship, reforming the asylum process, and addressing the underlying causes of migration. Harris believes that comprehensive immigration reform is not only a matter of justice but also essential for America's social and economic health.

The Humanitarian and Economic Implications of Border Policies

The debate over border policies is not merely a political issue; it has profound humanitarian and economic implications that affect millions of lives. Trump's and Harris' contrasting views on immigration represent two competing philosophies on how the U.S. should manage its borders, with each approach carrying distinct consequences.

Humanitarian Implications

Trump's stringent policies, including the border wall, family separations, and restricted asylum access, reflect an emphasis on deterrence. Proponents argue that these measures are necessary to dissuade illegal immigration and ensure that the U.S. can effectively control its borders. However, critics argue that these policies often disregard the plight of individuals fleeing violence, poverty, and persecution.

The family separation policy, in particular, sparked widespread condemnation from human rights advocates, who argued that it inflicted long-lasting trauma on children and undermined America's reputation as a defender of human rights.

The humanitarian implications of Harris' approach differ significantly. Her emphasis on reforming the asylum process, addressing root causes of migration, and creating legal pathways for undocumented immigrants reflects a commitment to humane treatment and international human rights standards.

Harris' approach seeks to balance security concerns with compassion, aiming to uphold America's legacy as a safe haven for those in need. By advocating for a more efficient and compassionate asylum system, Harris aims to protect vulnerable individuals while reducing the strain on the immigration system.

Economic Implications

The economic impact of immigration policies is another critical consideration. Trump's approach, which includes restrictions on both legal and illegal immigration, is based on the belief that limiting immigration will protect American jobs and reduce the economic burden on public resources. Supporters argue that stricter immigration policies prevent undocumented workers from driving down wages and that limiting access to public assistance for immigrants reduces taxpayer costs.

Critics, however, argue that these policies ignore the economic contributions of immigrants, who often fill essential roles in industries such as agriculture, healthcare, and construction. The restrictive stance also risks labor shortages, particularly in sectors that rely heavily on immigrant labor.

Harris' immigration policy emphasizes the economic benefits of a more inclusive approach. She argues that providing undocumented immigrants with a path to citizenship would allow them to fully participate in the economy, pay taxes, and contribute to Social Security and Medicare. Studies have shown that immigrants, both documented and undocumented, contribute billions of dollars to the U.S. economy each year.

Harris' focus on family reunification and expanding work visas aims to support economic growth by meeting labor demands in critical industries. By creating a more robust legal immigration system, she believes the U.S. can harness the potential of immigrants while ensuring fair labor practices and reducing exploitation.

Balancing Security with Humanity

At the heart of the immigration debate lies a fundamental question: how can the U.S. balance the need for border security with its commitment to humanitarian values? Trump's policies prioritize security and deterrence, reflecting a belief that strict measures are necessary to maintain national sovereignty. His approach resonates with voters who see immigration as a potential threat to American jobs, safety, and culture.

In contrast, Harris' platform seeks to strike a balance by implementing security measures that protect borders without compromising human rights. She advocates for reforming immigration policies to reflect a compassionate and efficient system, arguing that humane treatment of immigrants does not conflict with maintaining secure borders. Her supporters believe that America's strength lies in its diversity and that welcoming immigrants aligns with core American principles of freedom, opportunity, and justice.

The immigration policies advocated by Trump and Harris in the 2024 election represent two fundamentally different visions for America's future. Trump's approach is rooted in strict border control and enforcement, prioritizing security and reducing immigration to protect American jobs and resources. His policies appeal to those who view immigration as a challenge to national security and economic stability, believing that strict measures are necessary to preserve the American way of life.

Trump's proposals reflect a conviction that a strong stance on immigration safeguards American communities from perceived threats associated with illegal immigration, drug trafficking, and competition in the labor market. Supporters argue that by emphasizing border security, Trump is prioritizing the safety and prosperity of American citizens.

On the other hand, Harris' immigration policies underscore the belief that America's identity is deeply intertwined with its role as a land of opportunity and refuge. Her approach combines practical reforms with a humanitarian perspective, aiming to create a more welcoming system that upholds America's historical values while addressing the realities of modern migration.

By focusing on legal pathways, support for Dreamers, and targeted measures to address the root causes of migration, Harris' platform seeks to bridge the gap between security and compassion. Her supporters view her immigration stance as one that values diversity, equity, and respect for human dignity, essential qualities they believe strengthen the nation as a whole.

Overall, the debate over immigration policy in the 2024 election poses significant questions about America's future identity and values. Will the country adopt a more restrictive stance, emphasizing border security and limited immigration as a means to protect American jobs and culture, or will it embrace a more inclusive approach, recognizing the contributions of immigrants and providing new pathways to citizenship? This chapter highlights the critical stakes involved in this decision, as well as the broader implications for U.S. society, economy, and moral standing in the world.

AMERICA DECIDES *2024*

Ultimately, voters in 2024 are faced with a choice between two competing visions. Trump's platform appeals to those who prioritize strong borders and a cautious approach to immigration, viewing these as essential for safeguarding American interests. Harris' vision, meanwhile, speaks to those who see immigration as an integral part of America's national story, one that reflects both its history as a nation of immigrants and its aspirations to be a leader in human rights.

As the nation heads toward the election, immigration will undoubtedly remain a focal point of debate, not only for its impact on policy but for its symbolism in the broader narrative of what it means to be American. The outcome of this debate could shape not only immigration policy but the nation's values and identity for generations to come.

CHAPTER SIX

National Security and Foreign Policy - America's Role on the Global Stage

Donald Trump's foreign policy has often been characterized by a mix of isolationist tendencies and pragmatic realism, focusing on America First principles that emphasize national sovereignty, economic interests, and a skeptical view of international organizations. His presidency marked a significant departure from traditional U.S. foreign policy approaches, which often emphasized global engagement and multilateralism.

Central to Trump's doctrine was the belief that previous administrations had overextended U.S. commitments abroad at the expense of American interests. He criticized NATO allies for not meeting their defense spending obligations and called for a reevaluation of U.S. involvement in long-standing alliances and treaties. This stance resonated with his supporters, who viewed it as a necessary recalibration of America's role in the world, prioritizing domestic needs over international obligations.

One of Trump's hallmark policies was the withdrawal from several key international agreements. Notably, he pulled the U.S. out of the Paris Climate Agreement, arguing that it was economically disadvantageous and unfair to American workers. He also withdrew from the Iran nuclear deal, framing it as a flawed agreement that failed to prevent Tehran from pursuing nuclear weapons. Trump's administration emphasized a confrontational approach to Iran, implementing severe sanctions in an effort to curb its influence in the Middle East.

Trump's approach to China was similarly aggressive. He viewed China as a strategic competitor and sought to counter its rise through tariffs and trade negotiations aimed at reducing the trade deficit. The trade war with China became a significant aspect of his foreign policy, reflecting a broader skepticism toward globalization and a desire to protect American manufacturing jobs.

While Trump's foreign policy rhetoric often included themes of isolationism—emphasizing the need for America to focus on its own interests—his actions demonstrated a willingness to engage in unilateral military actions. His administration's decision to launch airstrikes in Syria in response to chemical weapon attacks underscored a complex relationship with military intervention, oscillating between isolationism and a readiness to exert military power when deemed necessary.

Trump's foreign policy has sparked considerable debate. Supporters argue that his approach restored a sense of realism and accountability to U.S. foreign engagements, while critics contend that it undermined longstanding alliances and international norms, leading to a more chaotic global landscape. As Trump seeks re-election in 2024, his foreign policy platform is likely to continue emphasizing national sovereignty, a critical stance on China, and a commitment to renegotiating international agreements that do not serve U.S. interests.

Harris' Diplomatic Vision: Collaboration and Multilateralism

In stark contrast to Trump's approach, Kamala Harris advocates for a foreign policy rooted in collaboration, diplomacy, and multilateralism. Her vision emphasizes the importance of international partnerships and alliances, viewing them as essential tools for addressing global challenges. Harris believes that America's strength lies not just in military might but in its ability to lead through diplomacy and to foster cooperative relationships with other nations.

Harris' foreign policy philosophy is grounded in the belief that global issues, such as climate change, pandemics, and terrorism, require collective action. She has argued for a return to international agreements and has expressed a commitment to rejoining the Paris Climate Agreement, emphasizing the urgency of addressing climate change not only as a domestic priority but as a global imperative. Harris' approach recognizes the interconnectedness of today's challenges, advocating for U.S. leadership in fostering multilateral responses.

Her stance on China reflects a nuanced understanding of the geopolitical landscape. While recognizing China as a strategic competitor, Harris emphasizes the need for diplomatic engagement and cooperation on issues like climate change and global health. She argues that addressing the challenges posed by China requires a multilateral approach, working with allies to ensure a united front on trade, human rights, and regional security concerns.

Harris also advocates for a foreign policy that prioritizes human rights and democracy promotion. She has criticized authoritarian regimes and emphasized the importance of supporting democratic movements around the world. This commitment reflects a broader ideological stance, seeing U.S.

engagement in global affairs as an opportunity to promote American values of freedom and equality. Her support for global democracy aligns with a tradition of American foreign policy that seeks to uphold human rights as a core principle, countering authoritarianism and oppression.

Furthermore, Harris has highlighted the significance of engaging with international organizations, such as the United Nations and NATO, which she views as essential forums for diplomacy and collective security. By advocating for a robust multilateral approach, Harris aims to restore America's standing in the world, fostering alliances that enhance both national and global security.

In the 2024 election, Harris' diplomatic vision represents a stark contrast to Trump's approach, framing America's role on the global stage as one of leadership through cooperation rather than isolation. Her supporters believe that a return to multilateralism will strengthen alliances, enhance global stability, and reestablish the U.S. as a moral leader in international affairs.

Key Global Issues: Trade, Climate, and Alliances

As the world faces a multitude of interconnected challenges, the foreign policy positions of Trump and Harris will significantly impact how the U.S. engages with key global issues, including trade, climate change, and international alliances.

Trade

Under Trump, trade policy has been characterized by a confrontational approach, marked by tariffs and a willingness to renegotiate trade agreements perceived as unfavorable to American interests. His administration's emphasis on protecting American manufacturing and workers resonated with many voters, particularly in the Rust Belt, where communities have been adversely affected by globalization. However, critics argue that Trump's trade wars have disrupted global supply chains and led to increased costs for consumers.

In contrast, Harris' trade policy would likely prioritize fair and equitable trade practices, emphasizing the importance of maintaining relationships with allies while addressing trade imbalances. She advocates for trade agreements that include labor and environmental protections, viewing these elements as essential for promoting sustainable economic growth. Harris' approach seeks to balance the interests of American workers with the realities of a global economy, focusing on creating jobs through innovation and investment rather than isolationist tariffs.

Climate Change

Climate change stands out as one of the most pressing global issues, with far-reaching implications for security, health, and economic stability. Trump's withdrawal from the Paris Climate Agreement and skepticism toward climate science were hallmarks of his administration, leading to criticism from environmental advocates who viewed these actions as a significant step back in global efforts to combat climate change. Trump's energy policies, which favored fossil fuel development, further fueled concerns about the U.S. role in global environmental degradation.

Harris' platform, conversely, emphasizes aggressive action to combat climate change, advocating for a comprehensive climate plan that includes investments in renewable energy, sustainable infrastructure, and emissions reductions. She views climate change as not only an environmental issue but also a national security threat, arguing that its impacts can exacerbate conflicts, drive migration, and destabilize regions. By rejoining international climate agreements and committing to ambitious climate targets, Harris aims to position the U.S. as a global leader in the fight against climate change.

Alliances and Global Engagement

The strength of America's alliances is another critical aspect of foreign policy that will be central to the 2024 election. Trump's presidency marked a significant shift in the U.S. approach to alliances, with his administration often questioning the value of traditional partnerships and urging allies to increase their defense spending. While his supporters argue that this stance holds allies accountable, critics contend that it undermines the trust and cooperation that have historically defined international relations.

Harris' vision for alliances emphasizes restoration and strengthening of partnerships, viewing collaboration with allies as essential for addressing global challenges. She advocates for a renewed commitment to NATO and other alliances, recognizing the importance of collective security in an increasingly complex world. By fostering cooperation with allies, Harris aims to enhance diplomatic efforts and build a united front against common threats, from terrorism to climate change.

*AMERICA DECIDES *2024**

Overall, the contrasting foreign policy visions of Donald Trump and Kamala Harris in the 2024 election highlight the critical choices facing American voters regarding the nation's role on the global stage. Trump's America First doctrine, with its emphasis on nationalism and isolationism, seeks to prioritize domestic interests, reflecting a belief that the U.S. must protect its sovereignty at all costs. Conversely, Harris' commitment to multilateralism and collaboration signals a return to a foreign policy that values international partnerships and collective action.

As the world grapples with pressing challenges, from climate change to geopolitical tensions, the stakes of the 2024 election extend far beyond American borders. The outcome will shape not only domestic policy but also the U.S. position as a global leader, influencing how America engages with allies, addresses global issues, and upholds its values in an increasingly interconnected world. Voters will need to consider the implications of their choice on America's future role in international affairs and its impact on global stability, cooperation, and prosperity.

*AMERICA DECIDES *2024**

CHAPTER SEVEN

Social Justice and Civil Rights - Defining American Values

Donald Trump's approach to civil rights and policing has been a focal point of contention throughout his presidency and continues to shape his political narrative as he campaigns for re-election in 2024. His administration has often been characterized by a "law and order" mentality, promoting policies that prioritize police funding and support while simultaneously pushing back against calls for systemic reform in response to issues such as police violence and racial inequality.

Trump's rhetoric surrounding civil rights issues often emphasizes the idea that law enforcement is under siege, framing protests against police brutality as challenges to public safety. Following the murder of George Floyd in 2020, Trump's administration took a hardline stance against the protests that erupted nationwide.

He labeled many of these demonstrations as riots and sought to position himself as the candidate of law and order, often invoking the imagery of federal law enforcement intervening in cities with rising unrest. His support for policies like increased funding for police departments resonated with voters concerned about crime and public safety.

Additionally, Trump's administration has faced criticism for its handling of civil rights issues, particularly regarding the treatment of marginalized communities. He has often downplayed the prevalence of systemic racism and has promoted the narrative that African Americans and other minorities should view his administration as a source of opportunity, highlighting economic gains and employment statistics without addressing the systemic barriers that contribute to ongoing disparities.

In terms of specific policies, Trump established the "1776 Commission" in response to the perceived bias of educational institutions, promoting a curriculum centered on patriotic education and American exceptionalism while pushing back against critical race theory in schools. This move has been viewed as an attempt to redefine historical narratives surrounding race and inequality, a stance that some argue undermines the significance of understanding America's complex history with race relations.

The former president's views on civil rights and policing evoke passionate responses, with supporters praising his commitment to law enforcement and critics arguing that his policies exacerbate existing inequalities and undermine the fight for social justice. As the 2024 election approaches, Trump's position on these issues will likely continue to be a defining aspect of his campaign, appealing to those who prioritize a tough-on-crime approach while alienating others who demand substantial reforms.

Harris' History and Policy Goals for Social Equity

In contrast to Trump's law-and-order approach, Kamala Harris has built her political career on advocating for social justice and civil rights. As the first female Vice President and the first woman of Black and South Asian descent to hold the office, Harris embodies a commitment to increasing representation and addressing systemic inequalities in American society. Her background as a prosecutor and California's Attorney General has shaped her perspective on justice reform, leading her to pursue policies aimed at promoting social equity and accountability.

Harris' approach to civil rights emphasizes the need for systemic reform in policing and criminal justice. Throughout her career, she has advocated for measures to address police violence, enhance accountability, and eliminate discriminatory practices in law enforcement.

She was a vocal supporter of the George Floyd Justice in Policing Act, legislation aimed at ending qualified immunity for police officers, banning chokeholds, and establishing national standards for policing practices. This legislative effort highlights her commitment to addressing the root causes of racial injustice in the criminal justice system.

Moreover, Harris has focused on broader social equity issues, including economic disparities and access to education. She has called for investments in communities of color, emphasizing the importance of economic empowerment as a means to combat systemic racism.

Her proposals include expanding access to affordable housing, increasing funding for education in underserved areas, and supporting small businesses owned by minorities. These initiatives reflect a holistic understanding of social justice that extends beyond policing, recognizing that economic and educational opportunities are essential for fostering equality.

Harris' personal narrative also plays a significant role in her approach to social justice. Growing up as the daughter of immigrants and navigating her own experiences with discrimination, she has articulated a vision for America that values diversity and inclusion. Her commitment to uplifting marginalized voices resonates with many voters who seek a leader who understands the complexities of race and identity in America.

As the 2024 election approaches, Harris' advocacy for social equity positions her in stark contrast to Trump's policies. Her supporters view her as a champion of change, seeking to dismantle systemic barriers and promote a more inclusive society. The focus on civil rights and social justice will likely be a central theme of her campaign, appealing to a diverse coalition of voters eager for progress in addressing America's longstanding issues of inequality.

The Future of Race Relations, Policing, and Equality

The state of race relations, policing, and equality in America remains a pivotal issue as the 2024 election draws near. Both Trump and Harris represent fundamentally different visions for the future of these critical areas, and their approaches will significantly impact the discourse surrounding social justice in the coming years.

Trump's policies, characterized by a focus on law and order and a reluctance to engage in comprehensive reform, may appeal to those who prioritize public safety over the urgent need for systemic change. However, critics argue that this stance risks perpetuating existing inequalities and neglecting the voices of those advocating for justice. As calls for accountability and reform continue to resonate across the nation, the challenge for Trump's campaign will be to address these demands without alienating his base.

On the other hand, Harris' vision for a more equitable society hinges on the belief that meaningful reform is necessary to dismantle systemic racism and promote social justice. The growing awareness of racial disparities in policing and broader societal structures presents an opportunity for Harris to connect with voters who are passionate about civil rights. Her commitment to advancing legislation that promotes accountability in law enforcement and invests in marginalized communities positions her as a candidate for transformative change.

The future of race relations in America will depend not only on the outcomes of the 2024 election but also on the broader societal shifts that continue to evolve. The Black Lives Matter movement and other social justice initiatives have sparked conversations about racial equity, prompting many Americans to engage with these issues in new ways. As the nation grapples with its history and the present realities of systemic racism, the electoral choices made in 2024 will significantly influence the trajectory of these discussions.

In conclusion, the 2024 election presents a defining moment for America's values, particularly in relation to social justice and civil rights. Voters will have the opportunity to choose between two contrasting visions for the future, each reflecting fundamentally different beliefs about the role of government in promoting equality and addressing systemic injustices.

The outcome of this election will not only shape domestic policies but will also have lasting implications for America's identity and its commitment to upholding the principles of justice and equality for all.

CHAPTER EIGHT

The Environment and Climate Change - Competing Visions for Sustainability

During his presidency, Donald Trump's approach to environmental policy was marked by significant deregulation and a strong emphasis on energy independence through the promotion of fossil fuels. His administration's philosophy was rooted in the belief that environmental regulations hindered economic growth and job creation, particularly in the coal, oil, and natural gas industries.

This deregulatory agenda appealed to many voters in industrial and energy-producing states who felt that previous policies had stifled their economic opportunities.

One of the hallmark actions of Trump's environmental policy was the rollback of numerous regulations established under the Obama administration, particularly those aimed at addressing climate change. This included withdrawing the United States from the Paris Climate Agreement, a landmark international accord aimed at reducing greenhouse gas emissions.

Trump argued that the agreement was disadvantageous to the U.S. economy, claiming it imposed unfair restrictions that would lead to job losses in key industries. His decision to exit the agreement was widely criticized by environmentalists and international leaders, who viewed it as a significant setback in the global fight against climate change.

In addition to exiting the Paris Agreement, the Trump administration targeted several specific regulations. For instance, the Environmental Protection Agency (EPA) repealed the Clean Power Plan, which sought to reduce carbon emissions from power plants, and rolled back vehicle emissions standards aimed at increasing fuel efficiency. These actions were framed as efforts to protect American jobs and promote economic growth, but they were met with backlash from environmental advocates who argued that they jeopardized public health and the environment.

Trump's energy policies heavily favored the expansion of fossil fuel production, including oil drilling in protected areas such as the Arctic National Wildlife Refuge and the promotion of coal mining. He sought to open federal lands to oil and gas exploration and championed the interests of industries that were often at odds with environmental protections. This approach not only raised concerns about the environmental impacts of fossil fuel extraction but also drew criticism for its potential contribution to climate change, as increased emissions from these activities could exacerbate global warming.

Despite the criticisms, Trump's supporters argued that his policies were essential for achieving energy independence and boosting the economy. They contended that by prioritizing domestic energy production, the U.S. could reduce its reliance on foreign oil and create jobs in the energy sector.

As the 2024 election approaches, Trump's environmental stance remains a contentious issue, with many voters torn between the perceived economic benefits of deregulation and the urgent need for environmental stewardship in the face of a climate crisis.

Harris' Commitment to Climate Change Action

In stark contrast to Trump's approach, Kamala Harris has positioned herself as a strong advocate for climate change action and environmental sustainability. Recognizing climate change as one of the defining challenges of our time, Harris emphasizes the need for urgent and comprehensive policies that address both environmental degradation and social inequities.

Harris' climate agenda is rooted in the belief that addressing climate change is not only an environmental imperative but also a moral one. She has articulated a vision for a sustainable future that prioritizes the transition to renewable energy sources, energy efficiency, and the protection of vulnerable communities disproportionately affected by environmental issues. Her platform includes ambitious goals for achieving net-zero emissions by 2050 and investing in clean energy technologies to create jobs and stimulate economic growth.

Central to Harris' environmental policy is a commitment to justice and equity. She recognizes that low-income communities and communities of color often bear the brunt of environmental hazards, such as pollution and extreme weather events. As such, her policies aim to ensure that the transition to a green economy is equitable and inclusive, providing opportunities for those historically marginalized in the economic landscape. This includes investments in renewable energy projects in disadvantaged communities, ensuring that the benefits of clean energy are accessible to all.

Harris has also advocated for rejoining the Paris Climate Agreement and committing to international cooperation to combat climate change. She views global collaboration as essential for addressing a crisis that knows no borders, emphasizing the importance of shared responsibility in reducing emissions and fostering sustainable practices worldwide. Her approach reflects a belief that the U.S. can lead on the global stage by promoting innovative solutions and supporting international agreements aimed at combating climate change.

In addition to her commitment to climate action, Harris has highlighted the need for comprehensive policies addressing the intersection of climate change, public health, and economic opportunity. She advocates for increased funding for research and development of clean technologies, as well as policies that support the transition of workers from fossil fuel industries to green jobs. By positioning climate change as a multifaceted issue, Harris aims to galvanize support across a broad spectrum of voters who recognize the urgency of addressing environmental challenges.

As the 2024 election approaches, Harris' strong commitment to climate action stands in stark contrast to Trump's environmental policies, presenting voters with a clear choice between two divergent visions for the future of America's environment. While Harris' supporters champion her efforts to promote sustainability and equity, critics may question the feasibility of her ambitious proposals and the potential economic impacts of transitioning away from fossil fuels.

Environmental Policy in an Era of Climate Crisis

The growing urgency of the climate crisis has elevated environmental policy to a central issue in the 2024 election. As extreme weather events, rising sea levels, and unprecedented natural disasters become increasingly common, voters are faced with the stark realities of climate change and its implications for public health, economic stability, and national security.

The differences between Trump and Harris' environmental policies reflect broader societal divisions on how to address climate change. Trump's emphasis on deregulation and fossil fuel development resonates with voters who prioritize economic growth and job creation, particularly in regions dependent on traditional energy industries. However, this approach raises concerns about the long-term sustainability of such policies in the face of mounting evidence linking fossil fuel consumption to climate change.

Harris' commitment to climate action, on the other hand, appeals to a growing number of voters who recognize the need for urgent and transformative policies to combat the climate crisis. Her focus on renewable energy, environmental justice, and international cooperation aligns with the values of those advocating for a sustainable future. As public awareness of climate issues continues to rise, candidates who prioritize environmental policies may find increased support from a populace concerned about the future of the planet.

The role of young voters in shaping environmental policy is also significant. Polls indicate that climate change is a top concern for younger generations, many of whom are advocating for bold action to address the crisis. As this demographic becomes more politically engaged, their preferences may drive candidates to adopt more ambitious environmental platforms. Harris' emphasis on inclusivity and justice resonates with younger voters who prioritize equity in climate action, potentially positioning her as a candidate who can mobilize this critical voting bloc.

AMERICA DECIDES *2024*

The outcome of the 2024 election will have profound implications for the future of environmental policy in the United States. If Harris is elected, her administration may usher in a new era of climate action that emphasizes sustainability, justice, and global cooperation. Conversely, a second Trump administration could solidify a more deregulated approach that prioritizes economic interests over environmental protections, potentially exacerbating the climate crisis.

In conclusion, the 2024 election presents a pivotal moment for America's environmental policies, with voters facing a fundamental choice between competing visions for sustainability. The policies adopted in the coming years will not only shape the U.S. approach to climate change but also determine the nation's role in global environmental efforts. As the climate crisis continues to unfold, the decisions made at the ballot box will have lasting consequences for future generations and the health of the planet.

CHAPTER NINE

Education and Workforce Development - Preparing America for Tomorrow

Donald Trump's administration took a controversial and often confrontational stance on education and workforce development, emphasizing school choice, deregulation, and the expansion of vocational training. His policies aimed to shift the focus of education from traditional public schools to alternatives such as charter schools and private institutions, arguing that competition would improve educational outcomes. This approach appealed to many parents and communities who felt underserved by their local public schools.

One of the hallmark initiatives of Trump's education policy was the promotion of school choice through the allocation of federal funds for charter schools and voucher programs. He argued that parents should have the right to choose the educational pathways for their children, which would incentivize schools to improve their performance.

However, this approach drew criticism from advocates of public education who contended that diverting funds to charter schools undermined the resources available for traditional public schools and disproportionately affected low-income communities. Critics also raised concerns about the lack of oversight and accountability in some charter schools, questioning whether these institutions truly provided a better educational experience.

In addition to school choice, Trump's education policies included a focus on vocational training and workforce development. His administration sought to expand apprenticeship programs and partnerships between businesses and educational institutions, aiming to prepare students for high-demand jobs in industries like manufacturing, technology, and healthcare. This initiative was framed as a response to the skills gap in the American workforce, where employers often struggle to find qualified candidates for open positions.

Trump also emphasized the importance of reducing regulatory burdens on educational institutions, arguing that excessive federal oversight stifled innovation and flexibility. He sought to eliminate or reform various education regulations, including those associated with the Higher Education Act, which governs federal student loans and financial aid. This deregulatory approach was met with mixed reactions, as proponents argued it would enhance accessibility and reduce costs, while opponents warned it could lead to increased risks for students and taxpayers.

As the 2024 election approaches, Trump's education policies remain a point of contention. Supporters laud his emphasis on school choice and vocational training as essential for empowering families and addressing workforce needs, while critics argue that these policies neglect the importance of adequately funding and supporting public education. The debate over the future of education and workforce development will be a crucial element of the electoral discourse, as voters weigh the implications of these competing visions for the nation's educational landscape.

Harris' Agenda for Public Education and Workforce Innovation

Kamala Harris' approach to education and workforce development contrasts sharply with Trump's policies, emphasizing the importance of accessible public education, investment in early childhood programs, and comprehensive workforce innovation.

Harris' agenda reflects a belief that quality education is a fundamental right that should be available to all Americans, regardless of their socioeconomic background.

One of the central tenets of Harris' education policy is the commitment to fully funding public education and expanding access to high-quality early childhood education. She has advocated for universal pre-K programs, recognizing the critical role that early education plays in shaping a child's future. By investing in early childhood education, Harris aims to address disparities that often begin at a young age, ensuring that all children have the opportunity to succeed academically and develop essential skills.

Harris has also been a vocal proponent of reducing the financial burdens associated with higher education. She supports initiatives to make college more affordable, including proposals for tuition-free community college and increased funding for Pell Grants. Her policies aim to alleviate the student debt crisis, which has burdened millions of Americans, particularly young people and families from low-income backgrounds. Harris' commitment to making education accessible aligns with her broader vision of promoting equity and opportunity for all.

In terms of workforce development, Harris emphasizes the need for innovative programs that bridge the gap between education and employment. She supports initiatives that enhance vocational training and apprenticeships, ensuring that students are prepared for the demands of the modern workforce. By fostering partnerships between educational institutions and industries, Harris aims to create pathways for students to gain practical skills and experience, positioning them for success in high-demand fields.

Furthermore, Harris recognizes the importance of addressing the changing landscape of work in the digital age. Her agenda includes promoting STEM (science, technology, engineering, and mathematics) education and encouraging diversity in these fields, particularly for underrepresented groups. By prioritizing STEM education and workforce development, Harris seeks to ensure that the U.S. remains competitive in a rapidly evolving global economy.

As the 2024 election approaches, Harris' education and workforce policies will resonate with voters seeking a more inclusive and equitable approach to education. Her commitment to fully funding public schools, reducing student debt, and fostering innovation in workforce training positions her as a candidate focused on building a brighter future for all Americans.

The Role of Federal vs. State Control in Education

The debate over the role of federal versus state control in education is a critical aspect of the discussion surrounding educational policies and workforce development. Trump and Harris represent two divergent views on this issue, reflecting broader ideological differences regarding governance and responsibility in the education sector.

Trump's administration favored a reduction in federal oversight of education, arguing that state and local governments should have greater control over their educational systems. He and his supporters contended that local communities are better equipped to make decisions regarding their schools, curriculum, and funding priorities. This approach aligns with his emphasis on school choice, as it allows for more flexibility in the establishment of charter schools and voucher programs.

AMERICA DECIDES *2024*

Critics of this approach argue that reducing federal oversight can exacerbate inequalities in educational funding and access. States with fewer resources may struggle to provide quality education, leading to disparities in educational outcomes across the country. Detractors emphasize the need for a federal role in ensuring that all students receive a quality education, regardless of their geographic location. They argue that federal support is crucial for addressing systemic issues and promoting equity in education.

On the other hand, Harris' approach advocates for a more active federal role in education, particularly in funding and support for public schools. She emphasizes the importance of federal investment in education to ensure that all students have access to high-quality learning opportunities. This includes initiatives to close funding gaps between wealthy and low-income school districts, providing additional resources to schools serving marginalized communities.

Harris' stance reflects a belief that federal involvement is essential for promoting educational equity and addressing systemic barriers. By advocating for policies that prioritize funding for public education and support for vulnerable populations, she aims to create a more level playing field for students across the nation. This approach acknowledges the disparities that exist within the current education system and seeks to implement measures that can help rectify these inequities.

As the 2024 election approaches, the debate over federal versus state control in education will be a central theme of the electoral discourse. Voters will need to consider the implications of each candidate's approach, weighing the benefits of local control against the need for federal support in addressing systemic inequalities. The outcomes of this debate will significantly impact the future of education and workforce development in America, shaping the pathways available to the next generation of students and workers.

In conclusion, the education and workforce development landscape in America is at a crossroads as the 2024 election approaches. The contrasting visions of Trump and Harris highlight the critical issues surrounding school choice, funding, and the role of government in shaping educational opportunities. Voters will need to carefully consider these competing perspectives, as the decisions made in the upcoming election will have profound implications for the future of education, equity, and workforce preparedness in the United States.

CHAPTER TEN

The Influence of Media, Social Media, and Election Integrity

Donald Trump's relationship with the media has been one of the most defining aspects of his political career. His presidency was characterized by an ongoing conflict with mainstream media outlets, which he frequently labeled as "fake news." Trump's combative stance toward journalists and news organizations has not only shaped public perception of the media but also influenced the broader political landscape in America.

From the outset of his campaign in 2016, Trump utilized the media as both a platform and a target. He often turned press conferences and rallies into opportunities to attack media organizations that he felt misrepresented him or his policies. This adversarial relationship resonated with a significant portion of his base, who viewed Trump's criticism of the media as a rejection of what they perceived to be biased reporting. By portraying himself as a victim of media scrutiny, Trump galvanized support among voters who felt alienated by traditional news sources.

Trump's approach to media extended beyond mere rhetoric; he actively cultivated alternative media platforms and engaged with audiences through social media, particularly Twitter. His adept use of social media allowed him to bypass traditional media gatekeepers, delivering his messages directly to supporters and maintaining control over his narrative. This strategy proved effective, enabling him to rally his base and mobilize support through viral posts and hashtags.

However, the consequences of Trump's media strategy were far-reaching. His relentless attacks on the press have contributed to a broader erosion of trust in journalism, leading to a polarized media landscape where partisan outlets thrive. Many Americans now rely on news sources that align with their political beliefs, further entrenching divisions within the electorate. The 2024 election will test the boundaries of this relationship, as candidates navigate an increasingly fragmented media environment where misinformation and sensationalism can sway public opinion.

As Trump continues to campaign, his interactions with the media will likely remain contentious. The question of how candidates engage with the press and utilize media platforms will be pivotal in shaping electoral outcomes and influencing public discourse leading up to the election.

Harris' Media Strategy and Public Engagement

In contrast to Trump's confrontational approach, Kamala Harris has sought to foster a more collaborative relationship with the media. Recognizing the importance of communication in shaping public perception, Harris' media strategy emphasizes transparency, accessibility, and engagement with diverse audiences.

Harris' approach includes a focus on using media to amplify her policy priorities and connect with voters on a personal level. She often shares her personal story and experiences, aiming to resonate with constituents who may feel disconnected from traditional political narratives. By humanizing her candidacy and emphasizing empathy, Harris seeks to create an emotional connection with voters, reinforcing her commitment to addressing their concerns.

In addition to traditional media appearances, Harris has effectively utilized social media platforms to engage with younger voters and marginalized communities. Her social media strategy incorporates visual storytelling, highlighting her policy initiatives and community outreach efforts. By leveraging platforms like Instagram, Twitter, and TikTok, Harris aims to reach diverse demographics and foster a sense of inclusivity in her campaign.

Harris' media strategy also emphasizes the importance of accountability and fact-based communication. She has made it a priority to address misinformation directly, challenging false narratives and promoting accurate information about her policies. This proactive approach seeks to counter the prevailing climate of distrust in media and combat the spread of disinformation, particularly as the election approaches.

As the 2024 election unfolds, Harris' media strategy will play a crucial role in shaping her public image and voter engagement. By fostering a more positive relationship with the media and leveraging digital platforms, she aims to present a compelling alternative to the combative style associated with Trump, appealing to voters who prioritize integrity and transparency in leadership.

Safeguarding Democracy: Election Security and Misinformation

The integrity of the electoral process has become a paramount concern in the context of the 2024 election. With the rise of misinformation, disinformation, and foreign interference, candidates must navigate a complex landscape that poses significant challenges to democratic processes.

Both Trump and Harris have addressed the issue of election integrity, albeit from different perspectives. Trump's repeated claims of widespread voter fraud during the 2020 election have fueled concerns about the legitimacy of electoral outcomes. His rhetoric has led to the implementation of stricter voting laws in several states, aimed at addressing perceived vulnerabilities in the electoral system. However, critics argue that these laws disproportionately affect marginalized communities and undermine access to the ballot box.

On the other hand, Harris has emphasized the need to protect voting rights and safeguard democracy against misinformation. She has called for comprehensive reforms to ensure that all

AMERICA DECIDES *2024*

Americans can participate in the electoral process without facing barriers. This includes advocating for the expansion of early voting, mail-in ballots, and automatic voter registration to increase accessibility.

Harris' campaign also focuses on combating misinformation, particularly in the digital realm. With social media platforms playing a central role in shaping public opinion, Harris has advocated for greater accountability from tech companies in addressing the spread of false information. This includes calls for transparent policies regarding content moderation and the promotion of accurate information about voting procedures.

The challenge of election integrity is compounded by the growing influence of social media in political discourse. Both candidates must navigate the delicate balance between free speech and the need to combat misinformation that can erode public trust in democratic institutions. As the election approaches, ensuring that voters have access to accurate information will be critical in fostering a fair electoral process.

In conclusion, the influence of media, social media, and election integrity will be pivotal in the 2024 election. The contrasting approaches of Trump and Harris highlight the broader implications of media engagement, public perception, and the challenges posed by misinformation. As voters prepare to make their choices, the integrity of the electoral process and the candidates' ability to effectively communicate their visions for the future will shape the course of American democracy for years to come.

CONCLUSION

The Election's Implications for America's Identity and Future

The 2024 presidential election represents more than just a contest between two political figures; it serves as a crucial referendum on the core values and identity of the United States. As voters prepare to cast their ballots, they are faced with starkly contrasting visions for the future of the nation. Donald Trump and Kamala Harris embody divergent philosophies regarding governance, society, and what it means to be an American in today's complex landscape.

Trump's campaign continues to appeal to a vision rooted in nationalism, economic protectionism, and a return to perceived traditional values. His supporters often resonate with his emphasis on American exceptionalism, prioritizing the needs of domestic constituencies over international obligations. In contrast, Harris advocates for inclusivity, equity, and a more global perspective on issues such as climate change and social justice. Her vision seeks to redefine American identity to reflect a more diverse and interconnected society, one that acknowledges the complexities of race, gender, and economic disparity.

The outcome of the election will undoubtedly have lasting implications for America's political and social fabric. Should Trump secure a second term, his administration may further entrench the ideological divides that have characterized recent years, potentially exacerbating tensions surrounding issues such as immigration, civil rights, and economic inequality.

Conversely, a victory for Harris could pave the way for comprehensive reforms aimed at addressing systemic injustices and fostering a more equitable society. The election will serve as a defining moment in determining the trajectory of American democracy, influencing how citizens view their role within a broader national narrative.

Where We Stand as a Nation at This Pivotal Moment

As we approach the 2024 election, the United States finds itself at a critical juncture, marked by significant challenges

AMERICA DECIDES *2024*

and opportunities. Political polarization, fueled by misinformation and divisive rhetoric, has created a landscape where collaboration and consensus-building are increasingly difficult. Voter turnout is projected to be high, reflecting a renewed interest in civic engagement among citizens who recognize the stakes of this election.

The nation grapples with pressing issues such as climate change, healthcare, education, and social justice, each of which demands thoughtful solutions and collective action. The COVID-19 pandemic has exposed vulnerabilities in public health and economic systems, prompting calls for reform and innovation. Citizens are more aware than ever of the interconnectedness of global and local issues, and they are seeking leaders who will address these challenges with integrity and foresight.

At this moment, the electorate is also contending with the ramifications of previous elections, particularly the long-term effects of Trump's presidency. The rise of populism, shifts in party dynamics, and evolving demographics all play a role in shaping the political landscape. Voters are tasked with not only considering the candidates' platforms but also reflecting on their values and aspirations for the future.

Looking Beyond 2024: The Long-Term Effects on America's Path

Regardless of the election's outcome, the 2024 presidential race will undoubtedly influence America's trajectory for years to come. The decisions made in this election will have implications that extend far beyond policy initiatives; they will shape the narratives that define the nation and its role in the world.

Should Trump be reelected, his administration is likely to pursue a continuation of policies that prioritize deregulation, limited government intervention, and a confrontational stance toward perceived adversaries. This could solidify a more isolationist approach to foreign policy, impacting America's alliances and global standing. Additionally, a second Trump term may intensify ongoing culture wars and deepen divisions within the country, posing challenges for future leaders attempting to unite a fragmented electorate.

On the other hand, a Harris victory may signal a shift toward progressive reforms that prioritize social equity, environmental sustainability, and inclusive governance. The potential for a new administration to address systemic injustices and foster collaboration among diverse communities could reshape America's identity, reflecting a more equitable and just society. However, such reforms will require overcoming entrenched opposition and building consensus across party lines.

Moreover, the 2024 election will set the stage for future political movements and the emergence of new leaders. As the nation navigates the complexities of a rapidly changing world, the values and priorities expressed by voters in this election will inform the direction of political discourse and policy-making for decades to come.

In conclusion, the 2024 presidential election is not merely a choice between two candidates; it is a pivotal moment in which Americans will reaffirm their values, priorities, and vision for the future. The implications of this election will resonate far beyond Election Day, influencing the course of the nation and shaping the identity of America for generations to come.

As the country stands at this crossroads, the choices made will determine how America addresses its challenges and aspires to fulfill its promise as a land of opportunity, justice, and democracy.

Printed in the USA
CPSIA information can be obtained
at www.ICGtesting.com
CBHW050625201124
17649CB00038B/481